Dan E. Berry

Rom 1:16-17

THE POWER OF GOD'S WORD

The writing of this book was given to me by the grace of God. It is now my privilege to pass it on to you as a gift, free of any charge or obligation. It would, however, give me great pleasure for you to make a donation of any amount to one of the following four worthy Christian causes:

- Eastern Pregnancy Information Clinic
  P.O. Box 1838, Kinston, NC 28502
- The GATE of Lenoir County
  P.O. Box 638, Kinston, NC 28502
- Son Set Ministries (for The Refuge)
  1380 Lower Field Road, Ayden, NC 28513
- The Salvation Army (for use in Kinston, NC)
  P.O. Box 1479, Kinston, NC 28503-1479

DAN E. PERRY, ATTORNEY
P.O. BOX 1475 | KINSTON, NC 28503-1475

THE POWER SERIES

THE POWER OF GOD'S WORD

Understanding Biblical Truth

Dan E. Perry

CHAPEL HILL
PRESS, INC.

All Bible verses are from the New King James Version, except where
New Living Translation (NLT) or other versions are referenced.
All references to the New Living Translation (NLT) are
from the *Life Application Study Bible*.
NOTE: Italics or bold print within quotes or Scripture
citations indicate emphasis added by the author.

ISBN 978-1-59715-201-3

First Printing

This book is dedicated to my dear wife of over fifty-six years, Margaret, and my sister-in-law, Barbara Ruth Perry, both of whom continue to have a big influence on my life. They both love God's Word and study it daily, and have been weekly prayer partners for many years.

CONTENTS

ACKNOWLEDGMENTS

I am most appreciative of the kind comments many readers have passed along to me about my books. Whatever good there is in any of them, I can take no credit. It is only through the power and inspiration of the indwelling Holy Spirit that I can accomplish anything.

Humanly speaking, I am grateful for my dear wife, Margaret, for her editing, comments, and encouragement. I am also grateful for Barbara Ruth Perry, Rick Vernon, Gwen Gobble, and Jason McKnight for their time and effort in reviewing the prepress manuscript, and for giving me their constructive thoughts.

My thanks also to Linda Murray (typist), Edwina Woodbury (publisher, the Chapel Hill Press), and Katie Severa (graphic designer), without whom there would be no book(s).

Someone has said that the Word of God is to the soul what food is to the body.

Just as food is vital for our physical growth, so is God's Word vital for our Spiritual growth. I'm convinced that a person's degree of Spiritual growth is dependent on his interest in reading, meditating on, and knowing the Truth of the Bible. Its importance has long been accepted. In fact, I remember—back in the third grade at Harvey School—our teacher, Claira Benthal (later to become Mrs. Francis Rasberry) told us that year end and year out the Bible has always been the bestselling book of all times. She said that when people talk about "this year's best seller," they are really saying, "Next to the Bible, this year's best seller is _____."

The question naturally becomes, what is it about

the Bible that makes it so appealing? There must be something more to it than being just a storybook of some nonfiction matter of interest. To me the answer is that the Bible not only *speaks* the Truth, *it is the Truth*. It is God's message of Love and Forgiveness to the world. It's His Love Letter to all mankind!

As the writer of Hebrews stated in Hebrews 4:12–13 (NLT):

> For the Word of God is alive and powerful, it is sharper than the sharpest two-edged sword, cutting between soul and spirit, between joint and marrow. It exposes our innermost thoughts and desires. Nothing in all creation is hidden from God. Everything is naked and exposed before His eyes, and He is the One to whom we are accountable.

What that's saying is that if our lives conform to the Word of God, then our word and life in the Day of Judgment will be acceptable to Him. So it can be said that the Word of God is not simply a collection of words from God and a vehicle for communicating ideas, it is literally living, life changing, and dynamic as it works in us.

"With the incisiveness of a surgeon's knife, God's Word reveals who we are and what we are not. It penetrates the core of our moral and spiritual life. It describes what is within us, both good and evil. The demands of God's Word require decisions. We must not only listen to the Word, we must also let it shape our lives." (*Life Application Study Bible*)

Here's what the writer of the footnote to Hebrews 4:13 (NLT) quoted above says about God and His knowledge of each one of us:

> Nothing can be hidden from God. He knows about everyone, and everything about us is wide open to His all-seeing eyes. God sees all we do and knows all we think. Even when we are unaware of His Presence, He is there. When we try to hide from Him, He sees us. We can have no secrets from

God. It is comforting to realize that although God knows us intimately, He still loves us.

David's well-known Psalm 139 focuses on four great attributes of God: **His omniscience** (His knowledge of all things), **His omnipresence** (His Presence everywhere), **His omnipotence** (His unlimited power) and **His holiness**, which searches the believer's hearts and destroys evil men. Read how David brings it all together in the last two verses of the psalm:

> Search me, O God, and know my heart;
>   try me and know my anxieties;
> and see if there is any wicked way in me,
>   and lead me in the way everlasting.

The Bible's Impact Is Immeasurable

In preparing to write this book about the Bible, I collected a file of testimonies of what others have said about the impact that God's Word has on their lives as well as on the world itself.

In the September 2017 issue of *Decision Magazine*

I came across an article wherein four highly respected Bible teachers were interviewed as to the impact God's Word has had on their lives. Let me give you a summary of what they said:

• For **Kay Arthur**—who, as many of you know, had been living a rebellious, immoral lifestyle when the Lord saved her at age twenty-nine—her transformation process took root when she read and began to understand Romans 9:25 and the fact that "He called her 'beloved' [His bride] when there was nothing lovely about her." Now at age eighty-three, Arthur is in her fifth decade of teaching multitudes how to study God's Word through inductive studies, books, and television and radio programs. "I have been absolutely transformed," she says. "I know that I know truth, and I know God. I understand His character, I understand His ways, I understand His power, and I understand His love and grace because I've studied His Word. I love and totally believe Matthew 4:14, when Jesus turned to Satan and said, 'It is written, "Man shall not live by bread alone, but by every word that proceeds from the mouth of God."'"

• **David Jeremiah**, as author and pastor of Shadow Mountain Community Church in El Cajon, California, marvels at how the Bible's sixty-six books—written by some forty different authors over a span of some fifteen hundred years under the inspiration of the Holy Spirit—cohesively fit together. "The Old Testament prepares you for the New and the New explains the Old," said Jeremiah, who published a Study Bible in 2013 that has been distributed worldwide. "Jesus is the subject and basically the red line, the crimson line of blood that runs throughout all of its books. *He's really the message of the entire Bible.* From beginning to end, the Bible reveals God's glorious plan of salvation for sinful mankind through the life, death on the cross, and the burial and resurrection of Jesus Christ. Scripture makes it abundantly clear that He and only He provides the one way to eternal life, and that we are to repent of our sins and receive by faith His grace and forgiveness as our Lord and Savior. God sent us His Word to bring us to Himself," Jeremiah said.

• **Tony Evans**, an African American author and

pastor of Oak Cliff Bible Fellowship in Dallas, said of the Bible, "*It's not only information about God; it's the voice of God in print.* It should lead to worship of its Author." Evans continued on the Bible, "It shapes how I look at anything and how I view everything. It's the grid through which I evaluate the good, the bad, and the ugly in my life and in my surroundings. It has been the foundation of my ministry, so I am totally consumed with its truth, its power, and its Author." Evans stated, "The Bible has influenced many of the songs we sing, and the money we print has recognition of God. *The Bible has dominated the influence of Western civilization, but when the Bible is marginalized, that civilization disintegrates.*"

• **Michael Brown**, an author, scholar, and radio talk-show host, said no other source of literature comes close to the impact the Bible has had on societies around the world. He noted that while the Bible has never been more readily available in much of the world, including many translations for free on smartphone apps and websites, *Biblical illiteracy is on the rise. Thus, it's not surprising that religious liberty* *is being threatened by courts and a culture supporting anti-Biblical positions on issues such as marriage, sexuality, and gender.* "Invariably when we see apostasy in the church, we see apostasy from the authority of Scripture," Brown said. "We act as if we know better than the Bible, as if we are wiser than God, and we begin interpreting the Bible through our morality rather than interpreting our morality through the leaves of the Bible."

Kay Arthur, Tony Evans, David Jeremiah, and Michael Brown combined have published approximately three hundred books, booklets, and Bible studies, but all four teachers know that their literary offerings and oratory messages have no lasting value apart from the Truth revealed in Scripture.

Kay Arthur summed it up well when she said, "If no other book were ever written or published but I had the Bible, I would have everything I need to know."

PART ONE

Understanding God's Word

- Background for Understanding God's Word
- Is the Bible Reliable? Can It Be Trusted?
- How to Interpret the Word of God

CHAPTER I

Background for Understanding God's Word

To understand *God's Amazing Love Letter* to us, we need an understanding of the big picture of God's overall plan and purpose for the universe. Let me give you five basic truths that I believe will serve as the background for our understanding of the Bible:

1. God wants us to know who He is and who we are in relation to Him.

2. Man himself is both physical and spiritual.

3. We live in two different worlds—spiritual as well as physical.

4. We were created to glorify God and enjoy Him forever.

5. The central theme of the Bible is Jesus Christ
    and Him crucified.

There is so much more to know, but these five
points will at least get us started. Let me elaborate on
each point:

1. God Wants Us to Know Who He is and Who We Are in Relation to Him

It is vital that we know that God is the **Creator,
Sustainer, and Ruler** of the universe and everything
in it. Here's what the Bible says:

- **Genesis 1:1:** In the beginning *God created the
  heavens and the earth.*
- **Hebrews 1:3** (NLT): The Son radiates God's
  own glory and expresses the very character
  of God, and *sustains everything by the mighty
  power* of His command.
- **Psalm 103:19:** The Lord has established His
  throne in heaven and *His kingdom rules over all.*

We can see from the Scripture that God is in

charge of all of life and everything that goes on in the world. But who are we in relation to Him?

We were created in the image and likeness of God with the potential for a strong desire to know Him and have fellowship with Him.

Our life's purpose is to glorify God and enjoy Him forever. The Bible spells it out:

- **Genesis 2:26**: Then God said, "Let Us [the Triune God] *make man in Our image, according to Our likeness.*"
- **Psalm 42:2**: *My soul thirsts for God*, for the living God. When shall I appear before Him?
- **Psalm 16:11**: You shall *show me the path of life*; in Your Presence is *fullness of joy*; at Your right hand are *pleasures evermore.*

2. Man Himself Is Both Spiritual and Physical

We've all heard of the familiar phrase *body and soul*. Back in my college days we all sang the popular song "Body and Soul," with the chorus, "I love you, body and soul." The meaning was simply, "I love you completely in your entirety," both inwardly (spiritually) and outwardly (bodily).

In my growing-up years, my general concept of life was that what you see is what you get. My best childhood friend was my across-the-street neighbor, Z.A. Collins. We were less than five weeks apart in age and we played together all the time, day in and day out. When we were together I saw him only as a little boy. He had distinctive physical features that I could immediately recognize as being my friend. It was some years later that I began to realize that what I actually saw was not the real Z.A., for there was something more to him than just his physical appearance.

I guess it was at the age of twelve—when I was born again by accepting Jesus as my Lord and Savior— that I really began to grow in the spiritual area of my life. There was something about the "inner man" that the Lord wanted me to know. It was not until I was well into formal Bible study that I began to ponder the real meaning and see the distinction between *the body* and *the soul* (which includes the spirit). I studied such Scriptures as those that talked about

- … piercing even to the division of **soul and body.** (Hebrews 4:12)
- For he who sows to the **flesh** will reap corruption, but he who sows to the **Spirit** will of the Spirit reap everlasting life. (Galatians 6:8)
- For to be **carnally minded** is death, but to be **spiritually minded** is life and peace. (Romans 8:6)

3. We Live in Two Different Worlds— Spiritual as Well as Physical

We have just pointed out that in essence you and I *have a body* that we can see, but you *are a soul* that we cannot see.

The real you is your human soul—the part of you that will live forever in your resurrected body, either with God or without Him.

It all depends on what you do with God's Son while you are on this earth. If you accept Jesus as your Lord and Savior, you are saved from the death penalty of your sins and will live eternally with Him in the next life. If you reject Jesus as your Lord and Savior, you will be destined for eternal damnation. Here's the way John was inspired to write it in his First Epistle:

> And this is the testimony: that God has given us eternal life, and *this life is in His Son*. He who *has the Son* has life; he who *does not have the Son* does not have life. (5:11–12)

Let me give you several Scriptures to help you see the difference between the way of Jesus (the spiritual world) and the way of the world system (the physical world). They speak for themselves:

- **John 8:23:** And He said to them [the Jews who sought to kill Him], *you are of this world; I am not of this world.*
- **John 16:33:** ... *in the world* you will have

tribulation, but be of good cheer, *I [Jesus] have overcome the world.*

- **1 John 2:15**: Do not love *the world* or the things in the world. *If anyone loves the world,* the love of the Father is not in them.
- **1 John 3:1**: Behold what manner of love the Father has bestowed on us, that we shall be *called children of God.* Therefore the *world does not know us,* because it did not know Him.
- **Romans 12:2**: And *do not be conformed to this world,* but be transformed by the renewing of your mind....

4. We Were Created to Glorify God and Enjoy Him Forever

From time to time we may wonder why God created us in the first place. Why did He even want to create the universe—and why did He decide to give you and me life with a body and soul, and to place us in an environment that is unique to all of us?

You may have heard it said that God created man to have fellowship with Himself, indicating that He was lonely. I must admit until recently I thought there was some truth in that. But the Bible does not support such a theory.

It is true that He *wants to reveal Himself to us* and He *wants to have fellowship with us*—but **not because He is lonely**. Wayne Grudem points this out in his *Systematic Theology*:

That if that were true [if He was lonely], "it would certainly mean that God is not completely independent of creation. It would mean that God would need to create persons in order to be completely happy or completely fulfilled in His personal existence." That makes perfect sense because the doctrine of the Trinity makes it clear that among the three Persons throughout all eternity there has been perfect love, fellowship, and communication. There can be no lack in any aspect of the Godhead. If there was any loneliness or lack of fellowship, God would not be the perfect

God He claims to be. God is self-existent, even before the foundation of the world, and does not need us or the rest of creation for anything. Yet we and all creation can *glorify Him and bring Him joy*.

God speaks of His sons and daughters as those "Whom I created *for My glory*" (Isaiah 43:7). Therefore we are to "do all to the glory of God" (1 Corinthians 10:31). As we glorify God and enjoy Him, Scripture tell us that *He rejoices in us*. "As the bridegroom rejoices over the bride, so shall your God rejoice over you" (Isaiah 62:5).

The *Westminster Shorter Catechism* gives us the bottom line: "The chief end of man is to glorify God and enjoy Him forever."

5. The Central Theme of the Bible Is Jesus Christ and Him Crucified

The *scarlet thread of redemption* runs through the entire Bible, from Genesis through Revelation. Some call it the *crimson thread of redemption* or the *red thread of redemption*. Whether it's scarlet, crimson, or red, it stands for the shed blood of Christ as payment for the penalty for our sins. The Bible is about how God chose to deal with man's sin of disobedience. Paul says that we all have sinned (Romans 3:23) and that the penalty for sin is death (Romans 6:23). Until something is done about it, we are in bondage to sin and to the kingdom of Satan.

God's answer to our sin problem is the death, burial, and resurrection of Jesus. It's our redemption through His blood sacrifice, and that was what Paul's entire preaching ministry was all about. He made it clear to the troubled church of Corinth, "For I am determined not to know anything among you except *Jesus Christ and Him crucified*" (1 Corinthians 2:2).

It was all in God's master plan for the universe. Wayne Grudem refers to the "covenant of redemption" as being an agreement among the Father, Son, and Holy Spirit, in which the Son agreed to become a man, be our representative, obey the demands of the covenant of works on our behalf, and pay the penalty for our sin, which we deserved to pay.

The Father orchestrated it all. The Son agreed to come (voluntarily) into the world as a baby, to grow into a man under Mosaic law (Galatians 4:4; Hebrews 2:14–18), to be perfectly obedient to all the commands of the Father (Hebrews 10:7–8), becoming obedient unto death, even death on a cross (Philippians 2:8). The Son also agreed that He would gather for Himself a people in order that none whom the Father had given Him would be lost (John 17:12).

The Holy Spirit in *the covenant of redemption* agreed to the will of the Father to fill and empower Christ to carry out His ministry on earth (Luke 4:1, 14, 18; John 3:34), and to apply the benefits of Christ's redemptive works to His people after Christ returned to heaven (John 14:16–17, 26; Acts 1:8; 2:17–18, 33).

It is interesting to note that this covenant among the Trinity was something voluntarily undertaken by the Triune God, not something that He had to enter into by virtue of His nature.

Remember, no one—no PhD, or however many degrees you have, or how worldly smart you are—**no one can begin to understand God's Word until he has first been born of the Spirit.** Only then does the Holy Spirit come into your life, so as to be able to open your eyes of understanding to discern the Truth about God and your relationship to Him.

Paul made this clear in 1 Corinthians 2:14:

But the natural man does not receive the things of the Spirit of God, for *they are foolishness to him*, nor can he know them *because they are spiritually discerned.*

CHAPTER II

Is the Bible Reliable? Can It Be Trusted?

Why is the Bible the bestselling book of all times? Robert Velarde has researched and written extensively on such questions as, How do we know the Bible is true? Is the Bible reliable? How did we get the Bible? How do I interpret the Bible? How do I respond to Bible critics? How do I handle Bible difficulties?

My Ryrie Study Bible and the David Jeremiah Study Bible (NKJV), as well as many other Bibles, have a wealth of information, including notes and articles, all designed to help us see that the Bible is indeed reliable and that it can be trusted in its entirety. One such book that I have is *Proof the Bible*

Is True by Ray Watkins, the subtitle being *Scientific Evidence That Proves the Point.*

Let me share with you a synopsis of all that I have read on those general subjects. For instance, David Jeremiah, who has faithfully studied the Bible for over forty years, says that "The Bible is the Word of God in words of man. The Bible is one Book—it has one ultimate author (God) and one storyline with a beginning and an end—but it can also be viewed as a collection of individual books with different authors, settings, and themes (all inspired by God Himself)."

The Theme of the Bible

While there are many subthemes of the Bible, such as sin, forgiveness, salvation, love, eternity, and the Trinity, *the overall theme is* **redemption.** At the risk of being repetitive, the story begins in *Genesis* with Creation and the **Fall,** and then makes its way through **Redemption** and **Restoration** (New Creation), ending in *Revelation.*

> The big picture of Redemption shows the kingdom of God breaking in—with God invading the kingdom of sin and darkness in order to rescue humanity and bring individuals into His marvelous light (1 Peter 2:9)

The Structure of the Bible

If you know anything at all about the Bible, you know that there are thirty-nine Old Testament (OT) books and twenty-seven New Testament (NT) books. It is interesting to note that in the same general time frame as the writing of these sixty-six Biblical books, other similar books were written, called the *Apocrypha*. But they are only considered authoritative by the Roman Catholic Church. Protestant Bibles contain the sixty-six books that were canonized by the end of the fourth century AD by the Council of Laodicea.

The thirty-nine books of the OT are collected into five subgroups:

- **Pentateuch** (*Genesis–Deuteronomy*)—Also called the "five books of Moses," these span the period from Creation to Israel's preparation to enter the promised land.
- **Historical books** (*Joshua–Esther*)—These twelve books cover Israel's entry into the promised land, the monarchy, the destruction of Israel by Assyria and Babylon, and the Jews' return from exile in Babylon.
- **Poetic books** (*Job–Song of Solomon*)—Also known as *wisdom literature*, these five books contain the collected poetry (songs) and wisdom from the psalmists and (primarily) King Solomon.
- **Major prophets** (*Isaiah–Daniel*)—These are called the four "major" prophets because of their lengths, not because their content is more important.
- **Minor prophets** (*Hosea–Malachi*)—These twelve prophets delivered shorter oracles in Israel prior to the northern kingdom's

destruction in 722 BC and the southern kingdom's in 586 BC as well as to the Jews who returned from exile in Babylon.

The Literature of the Bible

Consistent with the literature during the time its books were written, the Bible contains many different styles of writing:

- **Poetry**—While some books are all poetry (*Psalms, Song of Solomon*, and *Lamentations*), many other OT prophetic books contain poetry. The NT contains only a few examples of poetry (Luke 1:46–55, 68–79).

- **Law**—The Mosaic laws were the civil, ceremonial, and moral guide for the nation of Israel, summarized in the Ten Commandments (Exodus 20:1–17).

- **History**—The twelve historical books of the OT are the best examples, even though *Acts* in the NT is also considered a historical book.

- **Prophecy**—The twelve Major and Minor Prophets make up the bulk of this group, but prophetic utterances are also found throughout the first four Gospels and in the NT epistles.

- **Apocalyptic**—This category contains writings about the coming Day of the Lord and the end of the present age. Apocalyptic writing is found primarily in *Isaiah*, *Daniel*, *Ezekiel*, *Zechariah*, and *Revelation*.

- **Wisdom**—*Job*, *Ecclesiastes*, and *Proverbs* (and possibly *James* in the NT) are the best examples of books that focus on grappling with life in a skillful manner that pleases God.

- **Gospel**—The four Gospels that open the NT chronicle the life of Jesus and His message of the Good News of the kingdom of God.

- **Epistles**—There are twenty-one letters in the NT written by the apostles to new Christian churches. The author of *Hebrews* is unknown.

Who Wrote the Bible?

It is a generally accepted truth that Spirit-enabled men captured God's divine thoughts and words to produce an authoritative record of the story of redemption. The Bible was written over a span of some fifteen hundred years by more than forty authors from all walks of life—from kings to farmers, historians to fishermen, prophets to apostles. It was written in three languages (*Hebrew* [*OT*] and *Greek* and *Aramaic* [*NT*]) in four geographic regions—the Middle East, Mesopotamia, Asia Minor, and southern Europe. Some books were written and highly edited (like *Moses'* books and certain historical books), some were dictated to a scribe (*Paul's epistles*), and some were the result of scholarly research (*Luke* and *Acts*). The authors, inspired by God, withheld none of the failings of mankind, not even their own.

David Jeremiah sums it all up by proclaiming that the Bible has been the most influential book in world history, because its message originated with God and resolves the most pressing human need: reconciliation with Him.

What Does the Bible Say about Itself?

One of the most prominent verses about the Bible's own testimony about itself is found in *2 Timothy 3:16*: "All Scripture is given by inspiration of God...." Here the word *inspiration* is literally translated *God-breathed*.

2 Peter 1:21 confirms, "For prophecy never comes by the will of man, but holy men of God spoke as they were moved by the Holy Spirit." God superintended these human authors so that, using their individual personalities, they composed and recorded without error God's Word to man. We can conclude that inspiration does not involve mechanical dictation but the accurate recording of God's words.

One writer says that "inspiration is the process by which Spirit-moved writers recorded God-breathed writings." So it can be said that inspiration means that "human writers were inspired by God and moved by the Holy Spirit to record accurately what God wanted them to preserve." That doesn't mean the writers of the Bible were simply taking dictation. But rather it does mean that their words were *divinely inspired and recorded*.

The bottom line on which all Biblical scholars agree is that the Bible was written by real people, living in real places, recording real historical events, and also communicating God's real truths.

How Was God's Word Put Together?

As laymen, we may all wonder how the Christian Church ultimately put all the parts of the Bible together. Robert Velarde makes it clear that this question applies basically only to the New Testament, as the Old Testament was already accepted and certified in the books accepted by the Jewish people as divinely inspired. He says that following the *death*, *resurrection*, and *ascension* of Christ around AD 33, the fledging Christian Church found itself struggling for survival, and in the process, they wrote inspired documents that would later become the New Testament.

Velarde goes on to explain that the *process of canonization* has to do with what writings are deemed inspired and thus included in the New Testament *Canon*. The word *Canon* originated in reference to a measuring reed or standard by which something is measured. Of course, in reference to the Bible a Canon has to do with genuinely inspired writings.

Those who really study the formation of the written Word of God observe that several criteria were necessary in order for a writing to be accepted, but I mention only three basic ones here:

- The documents in question had to conform to the rule of faith, "conformity between the document and orthodoxy, that is, Christian truth recognized as normative in the churches."
- The document required some sort of apostolicity, "which as a criteria came to include those who were in immediate contact with the apostles."
- "A document's widespread and continuous acceptance and usage by churches everywhere" was also taken into consideration.

The Bible is inspired, true, and reliable. It is God's eternal written message of love and forgiveness to the world, and it can be trusted. It was God Himself who guided the process in accordance with His divine Plan. As such, the process of canonization was not left solely in the hands of fallible human beings. As Paul proclaimed, "All Scripture is God-breathed."

CHAPTER III

How to Interpret the Word of God

The Bible is recognized as God's written message of love and forgiveness to the world. We can call it *God's Amazing Love Letter* to us. He wants us to read it intently and meditate on its Truth. Read what Paul wrote to Timothy:

> Do your best to present yourself to God as one approved. A workman who does not need to be ashamed and who correctly handles the Word of Truth. (2 Timothy 2:15 NIV)

That's what He wants us to do: "correctly" handle the "Word of Truth." If we can't properly interpret

His Word we will surely become confused by misinterpreting and misapplying Biblical content. So the question becomes, how do we go about rightly interpreting God's Word? Let me give you five technical principles of interpretation that need to be understood. Don't be discouraged with the technicalities. Just hang on and persevere and seek understanding from the Lord:

1. **Hermeneutics.** That's a strange sounding word, but don't let it throw you. It simply means the underlying principle that can be applied to any written form of communication. In short, hermeneutics merely means trying to understand what the text is really saying. It involves our ability to make sense of what the Bible records. As Paul said in 2 Corinthians 2:14, "The natural man does not receive the things of the Spirit of God, for they are foolishness to him, nor can he know them because they are spiritually discerned." In other words, unless you are truly born again of the Spirit, you are not capable of understanding the in-depth meaning of the Bible. That doesn't mean you can't understand the outer fringes of the Truth,

but it does mean (according to my thinking) that you cannot understand the full meaning of what God is trying to tell you.

God's Word simply doesn't make sense without the aid of the indwelling Holy Spirit. It's "foolishness," as Paul says. The question is, have you been born of the Spirit so that you can understand?

The Importance of Context

n my opinion the greatest principle of Biblical nterpretation is *context*. Although there are sixty-ix individual books in the entire Bible, they make up a cohesive whole wherein God is directly trying o communicate His Truth to us. Think in terms of ach passage having an *immediate context* as well as *broader context*. Many times the meaning of the mmediate context and the broader context are one nd the same. At other times the broader context gives us much greater insight as to the full meaning of God's message. Just make sure you seek out the broader context in relation to the immediate context. Therein lies the secret of understanding God's Word.

Robert Velarde gives the simple suggestion that Spirit-led Bible reading will lead us to ask the following questions: What is the passage about? What comes before the passage you are examining? What comes after it? It then becomes obvious that in order to understand the full meaning of the passage, not only is immediate context important, but also the broader context. The bottom line is, what does the Bible as a whole say about the subject?

A good example is the subject of *baptism*, and the question, do you have to be baptized to be saved? Mark 16:16 clearly says that, "*He who believes and is baptized will be saved*, but he who does not believe will be condemned." It's easy to conclude that if you "*believe and are baptized*" means that you've not only got to *believe* but you've also got to be *baptized* to be saved. But the broader context gives us the correct insight. When the keeper of the jail asked Paul and ilas, "Sir, what must I do to be saved?" they merely aid, "*Believe on the Lord Jesus Christ* and you will be aved, you and your household" (Acts 16:30). Other criptures confirm that baptism is separate and apart rom salvation. It is God's will that once you are aved you are to be baptized as an outward sign of the nward experience of salvation by faith. That's why 'eter told the believers at Pentecost, "Let every one f you be baptized" (Acts 2:38). Paul wrote, "For *by race* you have been saved *through faith*, and not of ourselves; it is *the gift of God*" (Ephesians 2:8).

So the broader context of salvation is that we are aved only *by God's grace through faith*. The full insight eveals that we are not saved by *our faith*, but by *God's race* **through our faith** in God's grace. There's a clear listinction that needs to be recognized to get the roader context of salvation. Salvation and baptism re two separate but closely related doctrines.

There are three other strange-sounding words, eing related principles of interpretation, in addi- ion to *hermeneutics*. Velarde mentions them as being xegesis, *eisogesis*, and *perspicuity*. Again, I mention these as being technical categories of interpretation that I attempt to explain with help from Velarde:

2. **Exegesis**. In relation to the Bible, exegesis has to do with reading and interpreting the text by drawing out from it what God is actually trying to communicate to us. This is the right way to approach a passage, as we seek to determine what the God-inspired human author intended. It means looking at the text to see what it really says and means. On the other hand, *eisogesis* is the wrong approach.

3. **Eisogesis** can be defined as a reading of one's ideas into a passage of the Bible. It can lead to many errors, especially if we approach a passage with assumptions or presuppositions that really aren't in the text at all. It can be said that the "Golden rule" of interpretation is to seek to interpret a text as others would seek to interpret what you have written or said. This means that you would not want someone reading their ideas into what you have said or written that are not there at all. And so we should not seek to do this with Biblical writings either.

4. **Perspicuity (Bible clarity).** This term means that the Bible is always clear when it comes to communicating truths about the *essentials of the faith*. Here, Velarde explains that "There are no great secrets, hidden or esoteric interpretations that will grant us additional clarity when it comes to essentials of clarity." As Jesus said, "I have spoken openly to the world.... I always taught in the synagogues or at the temple, where all the Jews come together. I said nothing in secret" (John 18:20).

This brings up an important point about interpreting *essentials* of the faith (primary matters) as opposed to *nonessentials* (secondary matters).

We should be careful to ask ourselves this question: will my interpretation of a particular subject matter cause harm and division in the church to an essential doctrine such as the *deity of Christ, the resurrection, the atonement,* etc.?

That's the time we should keep in mind the broader Biblical teaching on the subject by consulting resources you can count on as being reliable and trustworthy. Among my most trusted resources are the *Believer's Bible Commentary by William MacDonald* and the *Moody Bible Commentary* by the faculty of the Moody Bible Institute with general editors Michael Rydelnick and Michael Vanlandingham. Also I have complete confidence in Wayne Grudem and his 1290-page *Systematic Theology*, as well as the preaching and writings of David Jeremiah, Charles Stanley, Warren Wiersbe, Jack Graham, Adrian Rogers, and Michael Youssef. Locally speaking in the Kinston area I call mostly on my wife, Margaret; Barbara Ruth Perry; Jason McKnight; and Dr. Rob McArthur. In fact, those four have reviewed all or most of my prepress manuscripts in the Power Series, because I trust their input and constructive criticism.

5. **Literal or figurative interpretation?** Both of these approaches are valued as long as they are judiciously employed. When Jesus said that He is the

"door" or "gate" (John 10:7–9), He is obviously not saying that He is a physical gate or door, with hinges and handle, but rather He is speaking figuratively. Also the psalmist uses figurative language when he says in Psalm 91:1 that God will cover us "with His feathers." We know that God does not have literal feathers. On the other hand when Biblical writers share about the resurrection of Jesus they do so quite literally, instead of a figurative symbol of some kind. Biblical text is clear that the resurrection is considered as literal. Paul acknowledges this when he writes, "And if Christ is not risen, your faith is futile; you are still in your sins!" (1 Corinthians 15:17). So we can see that it is essential that we understand when the Bible is speaking *figuratively* as opposed to *literally*. Knowing the overall context will help us understand what God truly means to convey.

If you are a born-again Christian, you are called upon to correctly handle and interpret God's Word and to "Be diligent to present yourself approved to God, a worker who does not need to be ashamed, *rightly dividing the Word of Truth*" (2 Timothy 2:15).

PART TWO

The Three Basic Biblical Doctrines of the Christian Life

- The Doctrine of Justification
- The Doctrine of Sanctification
- The Doctrine of Glorification

CHAPTER IV

The Doctrine of Justification

When we think of the phrase *Doctrines of the Bible*, we're generally talking about principles or tenets. More specifically, we're referring to a body of theological teachings that reveal God's mind on subjects that are intended to be adhered to.

I have come to understand that the Bible as a whole is simply a body of Truths written by holy men of God, by and through His inspiration and direction. It is written to a sinful, lost, and dying world.

God's purpose is to *help us see the Truth* about Himself as the sovereign Triune God of the universe, as well as all mankind, in relation to Himself. His further purpose is to lovingly offer us the way of salvation—**the Way** and **the only Way** for us to be saved from our sins and His coming Judgment.

A Synopsis of Biblical Doctrine

Most in-depth Bibles include a wealth of additional information, such as a concordance and a topical index of Scripture. My Ryrie Study Bible has a Synopsis of Bible Scripture that outlines many of the most significant doctrines of the Bible. Let me share with you a general smattering of the doctrines so that you can get a picture of overall Biblical Truth and purpose:

- **The Doctrine of Creation**—The coming into being of all things.
- **The Doctrine of Scripture**—Revelation, inspiration, canonicity, illumination, and interpretation.
- **The Doctrine of God**—Attributes of God,

the decrees of God (foreknowledge, predestination, election), the Trinity.

- **The Doctrine of Christ**—His preexistence, His humanity, His deity, His preaching, His passion, the Kenosis (emptying of Himself), His impeccability, His death, His resurrection, His ascension, His present ministry, His return.
- **The Doctrine of the Holy Spirit**—His personality, His deity, His characteristics, His works, His equal association with the Father and Son, the Work of the Spirit in salvation (conviction of the Holy Spirit), resurrection, indwelling, baptizing, sealing.
- **The Fruit of the Spirit**—His Love, Joy, Peace, Patience, Kindness, Goodness, Faithfulness, Gentleness, and Self-Control.
- **The Filling of the Spirit**—Being controlled by the Spirit.
- **Other Ministries of the Spirit**—Teaching, guiding, assuring, praying, the work of the Spirit in the future (in the Tribulation, in the Kingdom).

There are so many other Doctrinal Truths and teachings available for our pursuit of illumination and Biblical understanding, including

- **The Doctrine of Angels.**
- **The Doctrine of Satan.**
- **The Doctrine of Demons.**
- **The Doctrine of Man.**
- **The Doctrine of Sin.**
- **The Doctrine of Salvation.**
- **The Doctrine of the Church.**
- **The Doctrine of Future Things**—The future of the church, the tribulation, the millennium, the future judgments, the resurrections (the resurrection of the *Just*, the resurrection of the *Unjust*).
- **The Doctrine of Heaven.**
- **The Doctrine of Hell.**

As you can see, the Bible is God's Word of Truth. It's His written Word of Love and Forgiveness—it's His Amazing Love Letter to all mankind, chock-full of Doctrinal Truths. If you boil them all down, there are three Doctrines that emerge as being basic to all Biblical Truth and teaching: They are the Doctrines of **Justification**, **Sanctification**, and **Glorification**. Let me explain.

The Doctrine of Justification

I frankly don't ever remember hearing a church sermon on any of these Doctrines. My information has come through my own Bible studies and the ministries and writings of such Godly mentors as David Jeremiah, Charles Stanley, Warren Wiersbe, and others, including Wayne Grudem and his *Systematic Theology*. My further preparation has been to write down all the Biblical references to the related words *Justification, Justified, Justifies,* and *Justify.* It's amazing what you can learn simply by writing down what the Bible itself says about a particular subject.

Justification Explained

Justification occurs when God declares a sinner to

be not guilty. This happens when person trusts that Christ Jesus died on the cross in his place, to pay his sin-debt for him. He is confessing that he's a sinner, in need of a savior. He is admitting that he can't save himself, so he's trusting that Jesus and His blood sacrifice was sufficient in all respects for his salvation. God justifies the ungodly.

The Biblical word to describe this new birth condition is Justification. Technically, it means that the new believer now has the right legal standing before God.

The single most important question for all mankind is simply this: How and when do we gain right legal standing before a sovereign and holy God? Jesus Himself gave us the only true answer when He explained it to a seeking ruler of the Jews, a member of the Sanhedrin. He told Nicodemus in all candor, "Most assuredly I say to you, unless one is born again, he cannot see the kingdom of God.... Do not marvel that I said to you, 'You must be born again'" (John 3:3, 7).

Martin Luther and Paul Realized
the Truth of Justification

The primary issue of the Protestant Reformation was a dispute with the Roman Catholic Church over justification. Martin Luther was a lonely, dissatisfied monk, seeking and searching for the truth of the gospel. Once he came to realize and understand the truth that justification was by faith alone, his religious world was turned upside down. It was the transforming power of Paul's statement in Romans 1:17 that set him on fire: the just shall live by faith! Actually, Paul was quoting the Old Testament prophet, Habakkuk (2:4). Both Paul and Martin Luther discovered the dividing line between the Biblical Gospel of salvation by faith alone and the false gospel of salvation by works.

The natural man is tempted to think that he's got to do something to earn his salvation. Believing and trusting seem too easy. And yet, the truth is, it's not about earning and deserving, it's about believing and receiving. Someone else has described justification as "It's not do, try, and behave; it's done, trust, and believe!"

It's interesting to note that Paul clearly teaches that justification is an act of God that comes as His response to our act of faith. God "justifies him who has faith in Jesus" (Romans 3:26). Also "a man is justified by faith apart from works of law" (Romans 3:28). Elsewhere Paul explains, "Since we are *justified by faith*, we have peace with God through our Lord Jesus Christ" (Romans 5:1). Moreover, "A man is not *justified by works* of the law, but through *faith* in Jesus Christ" (Galatians 2:16).

Justification Is Similar to but Not the Same as Regeneration

Wayne Grudem defines regeneration as "a secret act of God in which He imparts new spiritual life to us." That's also what the term "being born again" means.

Jesus was emphatic when He told Nicodemus that the only way he could get to heaven was that "You must be born again" (John 3:7).

The truth about regeneration is that it is totally a work of God. For example, when John talks about those to whom Christ gave power to become children of God, they "were born not of blood nor of the will of the flesh nor of the will of man, but of God" (John 1:13). So it is that John is specifying that children of God are those who are "*born ... of God.*" Our human will ("the will of man") does not bring about that kind of birth, meaning spiritual birth.

It's easy to observe that we do not choose to be made physically alive, for we do not choose to be born physically; it's just something that happens to us. Spiritual birth is similar; it's just something that happens to us, even though the believer does choose to respond to God's effective call on his life. By the way, I'm still trying to fully understand the mystery of God's sovereign work in regeneration. Such sovereign work was predicted by Ezekiel some six hundred years before Christ when God promised that that there would come a time in the future when He would give *new spiritual life* to His people:

> I will give you a new heart, and put a new spirit within you; I will take the heart of stone out of your flesh and give you a heart of flesh. I will put My Spirit within you and cause you to walk in My statutes, and you will keep My judgments and do them. (Ezekiel 36:26–27)

I am far from being a seasoned theologian, but it seems to me that the basic difference between regeneration and justification is simply this: Although both doctrines are centered on the new birth experience, justification goes a step further by emphasizing the fact that when the new believer is regenerated (born again), *he is given the right legal standing before God.* He now has Christ's righteousness and holy purity indwelling him by the power of the Holy Spirit. In other words, *justification* explains and gives meaning to the term *regeneratio*n.

When you are born again, you are trusting that Jesus paid your sin-debt for you, through His death, burial, and resurrection.

God gives you a new heart and puts a new spirit within you.

You have been *justified by your faith*.

You now have right legal standing before God.

You are now qualified to live in heaven with Him.

CHAPTER V

The Doctrine of Sanctification

The Christian life is a matter of *birth and growth*. You can't be a Christian without being born again (meaning born of the Spirit). That's what **Justification** is all about, as I tried to explain in the previous chapter. Just as you can't grow physically unless you have been born physically, you can't grow spiritually unless you've been born spiritually.

What is **Sanctification** all about? It's about growing in Christ. It's about growing in the likeness of Christ. It's about maturing in Christ. It's a progressive work that continues throughout our earthly lives. It's been called a work in which *God and man cooperate*, each playing distinctive roles.

Wayne Grudem defines Sanctification as "a progressive work of God and man that makes us more and more free from sin and like Christ in our actual lives."

Five Differences between Sanctification and Justification

You can understand Sanctification better if you compare it to Justification. Here are five distinctions to give you a better understanding of each doctrine.

1. Justification involves your *legal standing* before God, while Sanctification has to do with your *internal condition*.

2. Justification is a once-in-a-lifetime event, while Sanctification continues throughout your earthly existence.

3. Justification is entirely God's work, while Sanctification requires your cooperation.

4. Justification has to do with your perfect position in Christ, while Sanctification involves your daily practice of living out who you are in Christ.

5. Justification is the same in all Christians, while Sanctification is greater in some than in others.

Do you see the difference? Sanctification is something that continues throughout the lifetime of a Christian.

> The ordinary course of a Christian's life will involve growing and maturing in Christ. It is growing in the likeness of Christ. It is something that the entire New Testament encourages us to give our effort and attention to.

The Three Stages of Sanctification

Wayne Grudem is one of my heroes as being a deep-thinking, analytical theologian. I like the way he supports all of his doctrinal discussions with appropriate Scripture and spiritual insight. Here's an outline of some of his thoughts on the three stages of Sanctification:

Stage One: Sanctification has a definite beginning at regeneration.

A definite moral change occurs in our lives at the point of regeneration, for Paul talks about the "washing of regeneration and renewal in the Holy Spirit" (Titus 3:5). This initial step of sanctification involves a definite break from the ruling power and love of sin so that the believer is no longer ruled or dominated by sin, and no longer loves to sin.

Let me highlight two Scriptures regarding Paul's teaching about Sanctification from his letter to the Romans:

- **Romans 6:10–11**: "For the death that He [Christ] died, He died to sin once for all; but the life that He lives, He lives to God. Likewise you also, reckon yourselves to be dead indeed to sin but alive to God in Christ Jesus our Lord."
- **Romans 6:14**: "For sin shall not have

> dominion over you, for you are not under law but under grace."

Paul says that Christians have been "set free from sin" (Romans 6:18). In this context, to be dead to sin or to be set free from sin involves the power to overcome acts or patterns of sinful behavior in one's life.

That's what this initial stage of Sanctification is all about: When you are born again (meaning regenerated), you are given the power (through the indwelling Holy Spirit) to overcome the temptation of sin. Before your new birth experience you did not have access to the overcoming power of the Holy Spirit. You were dead to His ruling power! Now you can be an overcomer!

Paul is trying to help us understand that when we received Jesus Christ as our Lord and Savior, we were given a new life. We are no longer slaves of sin, but we are now "slaves of righteousness" (Romans 6:18). That's the beginning point of our sanctification process. We are now free to grow in Christ. And that freedom encourages and challenges us to grow in the Christian life. Read Paul's admonishment:

- "Do not let sin reign in your mortal body, that you should obey it in its lust" (Romans 6:12).
- "… but present yourselves to God as being alive from the dead and your members as instruments of righteousness to God" (Romans 6:13).

Stage Two: Sanctification Increases throughout Life

We keep emphasizing that the Christian life is a matter of *birth and growth*. The first stage of sanctification is about our *spiritual birth*, while this second stage is about our *spiritual growth*—growing in Christ. It's a lifelong process of growing in the likeness of God's Son—becoming more like Jesus!

Paul's entire ministry was centered around those two themes *of* **birth** *in Christ* and **growth** *in Christ*. Just as you "once yielded your members to impurity and to greater and greater iniquity, so now [you are to] yield your members to righteousness for sanctification" (Romans 6:19).

Once you have been born of the Spirit, you are now a child of God—and His great plan and purpose for all His children is to grow in the likeness of His Son. In fact, Paul says God has "*predestined* [you] to be conformed to the image of His Son [Jesus]" (Romans 8:29).

Let me give you one further supporting Scripture to emphasize that fact:

> But we all … are being transformed into the same image [Jesus] from glory to glory, just as by the Spirit of the Lord. (2 Corinthians 3:18)

Being sanctified means we are progressively becoming more and more like Christ in our daily lives. We may not feel like it at times, for we all fall short of being who we know we should be. Paul makes this point in this familiar passage:

Not that I have already attained, or am already perfected; but I press on, that I may lay hold of that for which Christ Jesus has also laid hold of me. Brethren, I do not count myself to have apprehended; but one thing I do, forgetting those things which are behind and reaching forward to those things which are ahead, I *press toward the goal* for the prize of the upward call of God in Christ Jesus. (Philippians 3:13–15)

Paul is telling us about himself as well as what he wants us to know about ourselves: simply that we're not fully like Jesus yet (and never will be during our lifetime), but we are to press on to achieve all the purposes for which Christ has saved us.

I am learning that in my own power I cannot be like Christ. Rather, if I am to be like Christ, He's got to do it for me. That means He's got to live out His life in and through me. That goes back to the *Power of Letting* (the first book in this Power Series). I can't, but He can! My objective is to let Christ live His life in and through me. That's a lifelong lesson in itself. And every Christian should practice it if he is to live the Christian life on this earth.

Stage Three: Sanctification Is Completed at Death

The essence of your sanctification can be described as *becoming in practice what you already are in position.* Always keep in mind that sanctification is the process of becoming more like Jesus. The reason the sanctifying process won't be complete until you die is that you are still a sinner in the sense that you commit daily sins and "nothing unclean shall enter" into the presence of God (Revelation 21:27).

You may wonder, "Why do I still have sin in my life? When Jesus died on the cross He took my sins upon Himself and in exchange, He gave me His righteousness. If I have His righteousness, why do I still sin?" The answer is that He took your fatal Sin Nature from you. That was the Sin Nature you inherited from Adam that caused his spiritual death. Jesus delivered you from the *penalty of sin* because He paid your sin-debt for you. "There is therefore now no condemnation for those who are in Christ Jesus" (Romans 8:1). For you as a child of God, He is now in the process of delivering you from the *power of your daily sins* and their rule in your life. That lifelong process of deliverance is called *sanctification*.

Just because you are a Christian and you no longer have your old Sin (spelled with a capital *S*) Nature, that does not mean you no longer commit daily sins (spelled with a lowercase *s*). The difference in *Sin* and *sin* is referenced by John when he said, "If we say we have no sin, we deceive ourselves, and the truth is not in us" (John 1:8). It is also helpful to understand the true meaning of this familiar passage by Paul:

> Therefore, if anyone is in Christ, he is a *new creation*; old things have passed away; behold all things have become new. (2 Corinthians 5:17)

Some interpret "new creation" to mean "without sin." But that's not the context of the passage. "Old things have passed away" refers to the fact that our original *Sin Nature* is no longer active within us in its original form. It's still there, but something new has been added when you are born of the Spirit.

The new creation that Paul is talking about embraces the inclusion of the Holy Spirit Himself who indwells every believer. We now have the power to overcome the tendency to sin that the old sinful nature encourages.

It is not right for a saved person to say that his old habits, evil thoughts, and lustful looks are forever done away with. But it is right to say that the Holy Spirit indwelling the new creation in Christ gives him the power to overcome those temptations that the flesh and the world system promote.

As long as you live in your body of flesh, you will always have a tendency toward sin! Why is that? Because the flesh and the Spirit are at war. They are in constant battle each day. The good news is that the Christian has the Holy Spirit (the living Word of God [Christ]) as well as the Written Word of God (the Bible) to help him overcome the everyday temptations to sin (*sin* being doing anything that does not please God). Read what Paul challenges all Christians to do in his letter to the *Galatians*:

> **5:16**: I say then: *Walk in the Spirit* and you shall not fulfill the lust of the flesh.
>
> **5:17**: For the *flesh lusts against the Spirit, and the Spirit against the flesh*; and these are contrary to one another so that you do not do the things that you wish.

Paul's personal battle between the flesh and the Spirit is explained in detail in the seventh chapter of Romans. Like all Christians, he says his dilemma is simply that he does the things he *doesn't* want to do, and he doesn't do the things he *does* want to do.

Only when the Spirit is no longer encamped in our body of flesh will the daily earthly battle between the flesh and the Spirit be over. That event is known as the *physical death* of the believer. It is further known as the separation of the body from the soul (which includes the Spirit). Paul describes our physical death as "To be absent from the body and to be present with the Lord" (2 Corinthians 2:8).

CHAPTER VI

The Doctrine of Glorification

In one of my books (I can't remember which) I wrote about the **two** basic Doctrines of the Christian life as being **Justification** and **Sanctification**. That was before I realized the importance of **Glorification**! The Truth is there are not two, but three basic doctrines of the Christian life.

To put these three doctrines in brief perspective:

1. **Justification** means that we have established a right relationship with God through the new birth experience. That's our position in Christ.

2. **Sanctification** has to do with the practical side of the Christian Life, our putting into practice what we already are in position.

3. **Glorification** occurs when our earthly existence is over and we receive our resurrection body. That's the completion of our Christian growth.

Wayne Grudem helps us see the full meaning of glorification by defining it as follows:

> Glorification is the final step in the application of redemption. It will happen when Christ returns and raises from the dead the bodies of all believers for all time who have died, and reunites them with their souls, and changes the bodies of all believers who remain alive, thereby giving all believers at the same time perfect resurrection bodies like His own.

When we understand these three Doctrines of **Justification, Sanctification** and **Glorification** we will have a good understanding of the full Christian experience from beginning to end. Without glorification, our birth and growth experience is left dangling. We've missed the big picture of what our sovereign God is doing in the total lives of His children.

Glorification—Explanation and Scriptural Basis

Ever since the fall of man in the garden, God's eternal purpose has been to redeem not only the complete man but also all of creation, for all creation was affected by sinful man. The scarlet thread of redemption has been interwoven throughout all of God's Word, from Genesis through Revelation.

> When Christ redeemed us on the cross, He did not just redeem our souls and spirits. He redeemed the whole person, which includes the redemption of our bodies.

Therefore, as Grudem points out, the application of Christ's work of redemption will not be complete until our bodies are entirely set free from the effects of the fall. God's whole purpose of redemption is to return man as well as all of creation back to their original state of perfection for which He created them.

The Bible says that the redemption of our bodies will not occur until Christ returns and raises our bodies from the dead. Read how Paul describes this mystery:

> We shall all be changed—in a moment, in the twinkling of an eye, at the last trumpet. For the trumpet will sound, and the dead [in Christ] will be raised incorruptible and we will be changed. For this corruptible must put on incorruption and this mortal must put on immortality. (1 Corinthians 15:51b–53)

In the meantime, Paul says we are to wait for "*the redemption of our bodies*," and then he adds, "for in this hope we were saved" (Romans 8:22–24). When we receive our resurrected bodies it is called *glorification*. Paul says that in that future time we will be "*glorified with Him*" (Romans 8:17).

If you are a Christian, you have a lot to look forward to. You can look to the future with confidence, knowing that one day your frail, worn-out body will be resurrected. You will have a new body, free from all pain, tears, and turmoil. It's all according to God's overall plan and purpose for believers in His Son's mission of redemption since before the foundation of the world. But remember, our resurrected bodies suited for heavenly living are only for those who choose to accept God's Son as their Lord and Savior. Paul explained the big picture when he wrote,

> For whom He foreknew, He also predestined to be conformed to the image of His Son, that He might be the first born among many brethren. Moreover whom He predestined, these He also called; whom He called, these He also justified; and whom He justified these *He also glorified*. (Romans 8:29–30)

What a Day of Rejoicing That Will Be!

On the day of our resurrection, our last enemy (death) will be destroyed, just as the Scripture predicts: "For He must reign until He has put all His enemies under His feet. The last enemy to be destroyed is death" (1 Corinthians 15:25–26). What a day of great victory and rejoicing that will be when Christ returns and we get our resurrected, glorified bodies. Paul says, "Then it shall come to pass the saying that is written: 'Death is swallowed up in victory! O death, where is your victory? O death, where is your sting?'" (1 Corinthians 15:54–55). As Wayne Grudem says, "When our bodies are raised from the dead we will experience complete victory over the death that came as a result of the fall of Adam and Eve. Then our redemption will be complete."

What about Those Christians Who Are Alive When Christ Returns?

Let's go back and reread 1 Corinthians 15:51b–53 as quoted above, because therein Paul is telling us that when Christ returns, those who are *dead in Christ will be raised with a new resurrected, glorified body.* It will happen "*in the twinkling of an eye.*" He says, "We shall *all be changed,*" meaning not only those who are *dead in Christ,* but also those who are *alive in Christ,* which will be the time of His coming (the rapture).

All who are alive in Christ will be "caught up" in a moment, in the twinkling of an eye. "The dead in Christ will rise first" (1 Thessalonians 4:16), and those who are alive in Christ will immediately follow.

Paul says, "Then we who are alive and remain shall be caught up together with them in the clouds to meet the Lord in the air. And then we shall always be with the Lord" (1 Thessalonians 4:17).

All Christians Should Live in Eager Expectation of Christ's Return

All Christians should be encouraged by what God makes known through His Word:

> But if the Spirit of Him who raised Jesus from the dead dwells in you, He who raised Christ from the dead will also give life to your mortal bodies through His Spirit who dwells in you. (Romans 8:11)

When this book is published I will be well past my eighty-eighth birthday. What was once a strong and virile body has now been reduced to a much more weakened condition. Although I'm in reasonably good health at the time of this writing, I've had several health issues that are a result of the aging process. The good news is that the Lord has graciously led me to be able to look forward with eager expectation to my glorious future, rather than with dread and fear of what is to come. He has taught me that *I have a body but I am a soul.* When my earthly journey is over, my soul (which includes my spirit) will live forever in my resurrected body, suited for heavenly living with my Lord and Savior. All praise to Him!

The Bible makes it clear: "For our *citizenship is in heaven*, from which we also *eagerly wait* for the Savior, the Lord Jesus Christ, who will transform our lowly body that it may be conformed to His glorious body, according to the working by which He is able to even subdue all things to Himself" (Philippians 3:20–21).

I have learned that life is made up of stages. Just

because I am in one of the final stages of my earthly existence does not mean I should look at my life as nearing its end. On the contrary, I'm looking at it as the nearing of a *new beginning*—and I find that exciting!

Here's a special insight the Lord is giving me: **Everything in this life should** *be in preparation for the next life*.

As John Quincy Adams once said, "When you read in the paper that John Quincy Adams is dead, don't believe it, for I will be more alive then than I've ever been!

Dear reader, I'm praying that you will develop a daily habit of reading and meditating on the Truth of God's Word. Whatever stage of life you are in, may it be used to prepare you for your life to come. First, be sure that you trust Jesus as your Lord and Savior, and then look forward to your glorious future in His eternal Presence!

What Will Our Resurrected Bodies Be Like?

We all may wonder what our resurrected bodies will look like. There is no better source of the Truth than the Bible itself. The bottom line is that they will be reconstructed and suited for heavenly living—similar but different from our physical bodies, which are designed for earthly living.

The Apostle Paul uses the example of sowing a seed in the ground and then watching it grow into something more wonderful. He goes on to explain in more detail what our resurrected bodies will be like, as recorded in 1 Corinthians 15:42, 43, 44, and 49:

> The body is *sown in corruption*, it is *raised in incorruption*. It is *sown in dishonor*, it is *raised in glory*. It is sown in weakness, it is *raised in power*. It is sown a *natural body*, it is *raised a spiritual body*. There is a natural body and a spiritual body … and as we have borne the image of the *man of dust*, we shall also bear the image of the *heavenly Man*.

Let me explain:

- **Sown in corruption, raised in incorruption.** Our earthly bodies are subject to disease and death. When placed in the grave they decompose and return to dust. Our resurrected bodies will no longer be subject to sickness or decay.
- **Sown in dishonor, raised in glory.** A dead body is dead, certainly nothing glorious! But our resurrected body will be raised in glory, free from wrinkles, scars, the marks of age, frailty, and traces of sin.
- **Sown in weakness, raised in power.** Weakness increases with old age until death itself strips a man of all strength whatsoever. But in eternity we will have supernatural powers unheard of during our earthly existence.
- **Sown a natural body, raised a spiritual body.** We should emphasize that spiritual does not mean nonmaterial. The Bible is clear that we will not be disembodied spirits, but will have resurrected bodies of flesh and bones.

Our Bodies Will Be Like Jesus's Resurrected Body

After His resurrection, Jesus lived forty days on earth before ascending into heaven where He is now "seated at the right hand of God making intercession for us" (Romans 8:33). Jesus lived in His glorious resurrected body during those forty days on earth, mingling with His disciples and followers. What was His body like? To put it in perspective, let me give you two references as to what the Bible says:

- **1 John 3:12**: "Beloved, now we are children of God; and it has not yet been revealed, what we shall be, but we know that when He is revealed, *we shall be like Him*, for we shall see Him as He is."

- **Luke 24:39–43** (NLT): Jesus said, "Look at My hands. Look at My feet. You can see that it's really Me. Touch Me and make sure I am not a ghost, because ghosts don't have bodies, as you see I do." As He spoke, He showed them His hands and His feet. Still they stood there in disbelief, filled with joy and wonder. Then He asked them, "Do you have anything to eat?" They gave Him a piece of broiled fish. And He ate it as they watched.

Christ's resurrected life is a model for ours. There's so much we don't know. I'm certainly no authority on the subject, but the Scriptures seem to indicate that our resurrected bodies will be suited for life on earth as well as life in heaven, where Jesus is now seated at the right hand of God (Romans 8:33).

As Jesus was raised to come back to live on Earth as well as heaven, so will we be raised to live on Earth as well as heaven (1 Thessalonians 4:4; Revelation 21:1–3).

Randy Alcorn's book *Heaven* is considered an authority on the subject, and he explains all this in detail. I highly recommend his book.

John 20:19–23 tells how Christ suddenly appeared in the room where the disciples gathered with the door being locked (v. 19). Christ's body could be touched and clung to and could consume food, yet it could apparently "materialize" as well. I can find no hard evidence that we will have that same supernatural ability, but most Biblical scholars conclude that we will be like Jesus in that respect.

According to Randy Alcorn, once we understand that Christ's resurrection is the prototype for the redemption of mankind and Earth, we realize that Scripture has given us an interpretative precedent for approaching passages concerning human resurrection and life on the New Earth. Shouldn't we interpret passages alluding to resurrected people living on the New Earth as literally as those concerning Christ's resurrected life during the forty days He walked on the old Earth?

PART THREE

Making the Bible Come Alive

- Appropriating God's Word Starts with Meditating on It
- Benefiting from God's Word Starts with Developing a Life of Obedience
- Make the Bible Come Alive in Your Heart by Meditating on It!

CHAPTER VII

Appropriating God's Word Starts with Meditating on It

The first six chapters of this book are designed to help you, the reader (as well as I myself), see the value and worth of the Bible. I hope I've emphasized that the Bible is the greatest book ever written—and that's why it is the world's number-one best seller of all time. What makes it so special is that every word of the sixty-six books, from Genesis through Revelation, was inspired by the Creator God of the universe Himself. It's His Divine Letter of Love and Forgiveness to all mankind!

The basic message of all sixty-six books of the Bible is centered on the Gospel, the Good News of the cross and subsequent resurrection—that God sent His only begotten Son, Jesus, to pay our sin-debt for us, and that all who believe and trust in Him as Lord and Savior are saved from the death penalty of sin.

If you want to appropriate God's Word for your own use, you must not only read it, but more importantly, you must meditate on it and ponder what God is trying to make known to you.

The Message of the Cross Is Foolishness to Unbelievers

In Paul's first letter to the Corinthians, he emphasized that worldly wisdom, which the Corinthians prized so highly, is the very antithesis of the wisdom of God. That's why he said,

> For the message of the Cross is foolishness to those who are perishing, but to us who are being saved, it is the power of God. (1 Corinthians 1:18)

What Paul is saying is that anyone who reads God's Word cannot fully understand its message unless he is a child of God. Some would say, "But aren't we all created by God—aren't we all God's children?" That may sound right, but that's not what the Bible says. John makes this clear:

> But as many as receive Him, to them He gave the right to become children of God, even to those who believe in His name. (John 1:12)

In other words, if you are an unbeliever in Jesus, you are not one of God's children. However, the moment you believe and trust in Jesus' saving power, you are given the *right to become a child of God*. Thus the door of your understanding of the written Word is opened. Until then, God's Word is *foolishness* and considered no more than faulty worldly wisdom to the unbeliever.

Solomon Had It Right

King Solomon lived some nine hundred years before Christ and never knew Jesus personally. Yet God gave him the insight to know the Truth. Here's what Solomon said:

> The fear of the Lord
>   is the beginning of wisdom,
> and the knowledge of the
>   Holy One is understanding.
>   (Proverbs 9:10)

Earlier in the same chapter, Solomon admonished us to "Forsake foolishness and live, and go in the way of understanding" (Proverbs 9:6). He is reminding us that the starting point of all true wisdom is the *fear of the Lord*. The word "fear" as used here can best be understood as meaning "respect and reverence." Someone has said that he who has true knowledge of the Holy One can see more on his knees than others can see on their tiptoes.

I think of the phrase *appropriating God's Word* as meaning taking the Bible as being our own; in other words, not only understanding what it says, but applying it to our everyday living. And the point we just made is that unless you are born again of the

Spirit, you can't even begin to understand the true meaning of God's Word.

The question now becomes, how does a Christian go about appropriating the wisdom of the Bible and making it his own? How does he make it a part of his everyday living?

Developing Godly Habits Is Essential to Living a Godly Life

A Godly habit can be defined as "a recurring and often subconscious Godly pattern of behavior that is acquired through frequent repetition." Let me give you five Godly daily habits that will help you to live a Godly life.

1. **A life of prayer.** At first the disciples failed to understand why Jesus spent so much time in prayer when there was so much good He could be doing. Jesus knew the importance as well as the power of prayer in His own life. He set the example for all of us by frequently withdrawing from the crowd:

- **Mark 1:35:** "Now in the morning, having risen a long time before daylight, He went out and *departed to a solitary place*; and there *He prayed.*"

- **Luke 4:42**: "Now when it was day, He *departed and went into a deserted place* [to pray]. And the crowd sought Him and came to Him and tried to keep Him from leaving them."

Prayer is merely communing with God— talking to Him and listening to Him— seeking His will in all situations. Jesus made it clear: "I do not seek My will but the will of the Father who sent Me" (John 5:30).

Jesus uttered the perfect prayer when He faced the painful prospects of the cross: "nevertheless not My will but *Yours be done*" (Luke 22:42).

An intimate prayer life should be a priority because it keeps us connected to God and sensitive to His will. Do you have a devoted daily prayer life? I ask myself that same question!

2. **Prayer and thanksgiving go hand in hand.**
In studying Paul's epistles, I noticed he often links prayer and thanksgiving in the same breath. Here are just three examples:

- **Philippians 4:6:** "Be anxious for nothing but *in everything, by* **prayer** *and supplication*, **with thanksgiving**, let your request be made known to God."

- **Colossians 4:2:** "Continue earnestly *in* **prayer**, *being vigilant in it* **with thanksgiving**."

- 1 Thessalonians 5:17–18: "**Pray** *without ceasing; in everything* **give thanks**, for this is the will of God in Christ for you."

Praying with a thankful heart keeps the door of communication open before the Lord. Our attitude of praise and thanksgiving sets the tone for developing a strong relationship with our Father God. We are acknowledging Him as being in charge of our lives as we seek to develop the daily habit of praying with thanksgiving.

3. **Meditation on God and His Word.** Meditation includes not only reading Scripture but also pondering it, and seeking to apply what God says by asking Him questions and surrendering all issues to Him. The psalmist knew the value of meditating on God's Word. He sets a good example for us all:

- **Psalm 1:2:** "But his delight is in the law of the Lord, and *he meditates on it day and night.*"
- **Psalm 119:15:** "*I will meditate on Your precepts* [Your Word and Law] and contemplate Your ways."
- **Psalm 119:97:** "Oh, how I love Your law! It is *my meditation all the day.*"

Developing the habit of meditating on God's Word is a choice we make. From a practical view, I doubt if any of us can be so totally committed to the Lord so as literally to meditate on His Word "day and night" as the psalmist says he did. But at least he gives us a goal to shoot for. In my own life I find that the early morning hours are best suited for a routine of concentrating on reading and meditating on the Bible. The idea is to find a time and a place that suits your own personal needs and convenience.

4. **Dependence upon the Holy Spirit.** Every believer in Jesus is indwelt by the Holy Spirit. Being constantly aware of the Holy Spirit's Presence as being not only *with* us but *within* us is essential to our success in living out who we are in Christ. That's why Paul was quick to remind and encourage the Christian believers, "Do you not know that you are the temple of God and that **the Spirit of God dwells in you?**" (1 Corinthians 3:16). It follows that if you have the Spirit of Christ living in you, you have access to all of the fruit of His Spirit, which is "love, joy, peace, patience, kindness, goodness, faithfulness, gentleness, and self-control" (Galatians 5:22–23). By developing the daily habit of reading and meditating on God's Word, we will slowly but surely begin the practice of living out His Presence of *love* and *joy* and *peace* and *patience* and all the other nine fruit of His Spirit. That's why Paul tells us, "Be filled with the Spirit" (Ephesians 5:18). It

is interesting to note that to be *filled with the Spirit* is not a onetime event. "Filled" or "filling" describes an experience that needs to be repeated. Acts 2:4 says, "And they were all filled with the Holy Spirit ..." and describes the power of Pentecost and the birthday of the church. I am reminded of a comment Margaret's mother made one day as she realized her need to be refilled with the Holy Spirit each day. She said it was "because I leak." I can certainly identify with dear "MaMa," for I leak too—constantly, and need to be refilled every day. I'm also reminded of the song, "Fill my cup, Lord, I lift it up, Lord! Come and quench this thirsting of my soul."

5. **Increasing in faith toward God.** Our lack of faith produces fretting and disobedience. God wants to help us move from having *little faith* to having *great faith*—and that takes practice. The more we are in the habit of *practicing His Presence*, the more our faith in Him and His goodness will increase. One of the great lessons I am learning is that, when I *complain about anything*, I'm acting as if I know better than the

Lord how to run my life! I'm constantly being led to realize that "The Lord has established His throne in the heavens and His sovereignty rules over all" (Psalm 103:19). When I am tempted to fret, or complain, or feel sorry for myself about any situation or adverse circumstance I'm experiencing, the Lord is gracious to remind me that *He is in control.* In fact, He rules over all and is in charge of history.

The overall Truth of the Bible is that God is in control of everything! Everything that happens in the world, in politics, and in your life and my life, is either *caused by God* or happens under the watchful eye of His sovereign *permissive will.*

His sovereignty is our firm foundation for believing and trusting Him. The reality of God's sovereign will begins to make sense when we realize that "God causes everything to work together for the good of those who love God and are called according to His purpose for them" (Romans 8:28 NLT). Solomon offers this advice: "Trust in the Lord with all your heart and lean not on your own understanding. In all your ways acknowledge Him, and He will make your paths straight" (Proverbs 3:5–6).

What is a Godly Life, and how is it achieved? This is an important question because, as believers, we are called to live sanctified lives that are fully surrendered to Christ. Although we know that this is God's will for us and that He's working toward this purpose in our lives, we have a responsibility in the process as well. What we habitually do has tremendous influence on whether we will have a Godly Life.

—Charles Stanley

CHAPTER VIII

Benefiting from God's Word Starts with Developing a Life of Obedience

What does a *life of obedience* mean? It means seeking out God's will and obeying it—surrendering your will to God's will. It means trusting in the promises of God and giving up your right to your own self will. The bottom line: It means *surrendering your all to Christ*, for therein lies **victory through surrender.**

In the military world, surrender means defeat. It means giving up to the opposing forces and being held captive. But in the spiritual world it means being set free by giving your whole self over to the King of kings and the Lord of lords. As Paul said, it means:

Casting down arguments and every high thing that exalts itself against the knowledge of God, bringing every thought into captivity to the obedience of Christ. (2 Corinthians 10:5)

In the previous two verses Paul gives the background for his argument against spiritual warfare: "For though we walk in the flesh, we do not war according to the flesh. For the weapons of our warfare are not carnal, but mighty in God for pulling down strongholds" (2 Corinthians 10:3–4).

The strongholds Paul is referring to are spiritual in nature and not carnal or physical. These spiritual strongholds must be opposed with spiritual weapons and not physical ones. Paul sees himself as a soldier warring against the proud reasoning of man and his opposition to the truth and knowledge of God's Word.

We Live in Two Different Worlds

This is one of the great Truths I've learned, and am still trying to learn: *We live in a spiritual world as well as a physical world.* I've mentioned this before in several of my books, but I tell you again, for it is one of the basic fundamental truths needed for understanding who God is and who we are in relation to Him.

In John 17:1–26 Jesus prayed His *high-priestly prayer* in the Garden just before His crucifixion. He prayed not only for Himself and His own glorification but for all those believers who would eventually make up the church after His ascension. One of the key elements of His prayer was His definition of salvation:

> And this is eternal life, that they may know You, the only true God and Jesus Christ, whom You have sent. (John 17:3)

God wants all of His children to know the spiritual nature of God the Father and His Son Jesus the Christ.

Developing a personal relationship with the Father and Son and understanding who they are help us understand who we are in relation to them. It also gives us the necessary background and foundation to understand the role of the Holy Spirit in the lives of all believers. Before leaving the disciples' presence and ascending back to heaven, Jesus said that He would ask the Father to send back the Holy Spirit, not only to be **with** His children, but to be **in** them. Read the exact words of Jesus as recorded in John 14:16–17:

> And I will pray the Father and He will give you another Helper, that He may abide with you forever, even the Spirit of Truth, whom the world cannot receive, because it neither sees Him nor knows Him; but you know Him, for **He dwells with you and will be in you**.

This sets the stage for helping the disciples (as well as you and me) understand that we indeed do live in two different worlds: the spiritual world as well as the physical world.

In my personal life, it was when God revealed (as well as confirmed) to me the truth of Colossians 1:26–27 that I really began to understand the two-world concept. Paul refers to it as a *mystery* that was once concealed, but now has been revealed. Read his words:

> The mystery which has been hidden from ages and from generations, but now has been revealed to His saints. To them God willed to make known what are the riches of the glory of this mystery among the Gentiles: which is Christ in you the Hope of Glory.

Once it hit home with me that the Spirit of the living Christ was literally indwelling me at the center of my soul—it was then that I began to fully realize that the power of God's Word was mine for the taking. It was at my disposal. It was mine to appropriate for my personal edification, as well as for His glory.

I Am Learning That the Purpose of My Life Belongs to God, Not Me

In the same manner that God the Father had a purpose for sending His Son into the world—to die to save all believers from the death penalty of sin—so He has a purpose for you and me and all believers.

The great lesson we've got to learn is that, yes, He does have a divine purpose for our lives. The higher lesson is that this divine purpose belongs to God and not to us. That's why it's called a *Divine Purpose*. We might also call it *His Divine Plan*.

Our objective is to live in such close harmony with God that we can see our lives from His perspective. That's when we learn to let Him have His way with us— to surrender our will to His will, and to let Him live His life in and through us.

We call that *the Christ Life*, and that's His overall purpose for all believers. And that's the meaning of "Christ in you, the Hope of Glory." That's what Wayne Barber meant when he said, "I can't, He never said I could. He can, He always said He would."

I like what Oswald Chambers says in giving us the following perspective:

When we say, "What a wonderful personality, what a fascinating person, and what wonderful insight!" then what opportunity does the gospel of God have through all that? It cannot get through, because the attraction is to the messenger and not the message. If a person attracts through his personality, that becomes the appeal. If, however, he is identified with the Lord Himself, then the appeal becomes what Jesus Christ can do. The danger is to glory in men, yet Jesus says we are *to lift up only Him* (see John 12:32).

John 12:32 records the words of Jesus: "And I, if I am lifted up from the earth, will draw all peoples to Myself." So we see, it's a matter of lifting up Jesus and not ourselves. It's all about the message of Christ, and not you and me as the messengers. An even more effective way to put it is to say, "It's all about Jesus and not about me!"

Jesus Came to Fix Broken People in a Broken World

We live in a broken world, and all of us who live in it are broken. It all happened when sin entered a perfect world through the disobedience of Adam and Eve.

God sent His Son to fix and restore not only broken people but also our broken world and everything in it. In God's perfect timing it will all be made right.

Jesus first came as a Humble Servant to offer salvation to all who would believe. His second coming will be as Judge and the King of kings and Lord of lords.

Two questions arise:

1. **If you are an unbeliever,** Jesus stands ready to come into your life as Lord and Savior and to fix your brokenness. He comes only upon personal invitation. He won't force Himself upon you. You have to invite Him to come in.

2. **If you are a believer,** Jesus is indwelling you. You have been "born again" of the Spirit. You possess all of His fruit of the Spirit to help you grow in His likeness. Your job is to collaborate with Him in this sanctifying process.

Collaborating with God Requires Surrendering to Him

After birth comes growth, and that's what all of God's children are doing as followers of Christ. God has predestined our final outcome, which is "to be conformed to the image of His Son" (Romans 8:29). If you are like I am, you sometimes don't feel like you are growing spiritually very much. In fact, that's why someone has so appropriately said, "The Christian life is falling down and getting up, falling down and getting up, falling down and getting up, all the way to heaven." Lord, help us always to think in terms of *getting up in Jesus's name after each fall.*

There are three ways to live your life:

1. Waste your life—in worldly pursuits.
2. Spend your life—by worshiping the world's idols.
3. Invest your life—in Christ and follow Him.

To invest your life in Christ means to surrender your will to God's will. As my friend John Grayson said, it means to "give up your right to …," and you fill in the blank. Give up your right to self-control. Give up your right to whatever is controlling your life apart from Jesus Christ. Let Christ control and be in charge of your life. The question for all of us is, "Who is on the throne of your life? Your own ego or Christ?"

Our greatest hunger is spiritual hunger!

Physical bread sustains physical life. Spiritual bread sustains spiritual life. Jesus Himself is spiritual life. Read His words:

- **John 6:48**: "I am the bread of life."
- **John 7:38**: "He who believes in Me, as the Scripture has said, 'out of His heart will flow rivers of living water.'"

The psalmist says, "My soul thirsts for God, for the living God" (Psalm 42:2).

To satisfy your hunger and thirst
for the Lord, you must surrender your will to God's will; and
to do that requires that you give
up all rights to yourself and your
own will.

CHAPTER IX

Make the Bible Come Alive in Your Heart by Mediating on It!

Technically the Bible is already alive! We don't need to make it come alive. Read what the writer of Hebrews says:

> For the Word of God is *living and powerful* and sharper than any two-edged sword, piercing even to the division of soul and spirit, and of joints and marrow, and is a discerner of the thoughts and intents of the heart. (4:12)

So let's think in terms of how to make the *Written Word of God* **come alive in our hearts** so as to make it the major part of our daily living. Keep in mind we're not concentrating on the *Living Word* (Jesus), but rather the *Written Word* (the Bible). The Living Word of God, being Jesus Christ in the Person of the indwelling Holy Spirit, is related, yet an entirely different subject than the Written Word of God, which is the God-inspired, timeless book we call the Bible. Of course the Truth is that we should want to make both the Living Word as well as the Written Word the major part of our daily living!

So the real question we're considering is, *how do we make the Written Word of God come alive in our heart?* Let me suggest three things to keep in mind as we ponder that question:

1. **The Bible speaks the Truth.** The Apostle Paul wrote that "All Scripture is given by inspiration of God." He then goes on to say that it "is profitable for doctrine, for reproof, for correction, for instruction in righteousness, that the man of God may be complete, thoroughly equipped for every good work" (2 Timothy 3:16–17). I think a more meaningful translation is from the NIV, which says that

all *Scripture is* **God-breathed**. God expressed His thoughts in the form of words. He breathed them in a supernatural way and communicated them to men and led them to write them down for permanent preservation. Even though the Scripture Paul is referring to only includes the complete Old Testament in existence at the time, today's Biblical scholars all agree that we are justified in applying this verse to the entire Bible. In 1 Timothy 5:18, Paul quotes the Gospel of Luke as Scripture. Peter speaks of Paul's Epistles as Scripture (2 Peter 3:16), and Paul confirms that he used words given to him by the Holy Spirit. Thus we read in 1 Corinthians 2:13: "These things we also speak, not in words which man's wisdom teaches but which the Holy Spirit teaches, comparing spiritual things with spiritual." Also Peter confirms that the writers of the Bible wrote the message that was given to them by God: "Knowing this first that no prophesy of Scripture is of any private interpretation, for prophesy never came by the will of man, but holy men of God spoke as they were moved by the Holy Spirit" (2 Peter 1:20–21).

The first thing to keep in mind as we seek to make God's Written Word come alive in our heart is that all Scripture comes directly from God Himself. We know this simply because it is the whole Truth and nothing but the Truth according to the Sovereign God of the Universe.

2. **The Bible is a timeless book**. As mentioned in the Introduction, I well remember as far back as the third grade, my teacher, Ms. Claire Benthal (later Rasberry) driving home the point that the Bible is not just the book of the month or even the book of the year, but the *Book of the Ages*. She said it is the best seller of all times, because it came from God and is therefore an unchanging, timeless book.

Psalm 119, with its 176 verses, is by far not only the longest psalm but also the longest chapter in the Bible. Almost every verse deals with statements about the Word of God. It is referred to as the wisdom psalm concerning the law of the Lord—as *testimonies*, *ways*, *precepts* (orders), *statues* (decrees), *commandments*, *judgments* (ordinances), *Word*, *path* (the last "word" meaning promise or utterance). Three such psalms from the King James Version have this to say about the timeless virtues of the Word of God:

- **Psalm 119:89** says, "Forever, O Lord, Thy Word is settled in heaven."
- **Psalm 119:152** records, "concerning Thy testimonies, I have known of old that Thou hast founded them forever."
- **Psalm 119:168** states, "Thy Word is true from the beginning: and every one of Thy righteous judgments indwelleth for ever."

Adrian Rodgers writes this: "There have been emperors who have decreed the extermination of the Bible, and there have been atheists who have railed against the Bible. Agnostics have cynically sneered at the Bible and liberals have moved heaven and earth to remove the miracles from the Bible. There have been materialists who just simply ignored the Bible. *But the Bible stands. The Bible is settled in heaven.*"

3. **The Bible is like a treasure.** The Bible is not only a *truthful book* and a *timeless book*, it is a *treasured book*. It is God's treasure book, and we should appreciate it as such. It is obvious that if we don't appreciate the virtues of the Written Word of God, we're not going to have any desire to understand it. This should be our clear objective: to understand what God (its Author) is trying to tell us. It's His Divine Love Letter to all the world. His message is simple: God loves you, and He sent His only begotten Son into the world to die on the cross to pay your sin-debt for you—and all who believe and trust in Him as their Lord and Savior are saved from the death penalty of sin. In a nutshell it's about love and forgiveness and the giving of eternal life to all believers in God's Son.

"Jesus loves me, this I know, for the Bible tells me so." You probably sang that childhood song as I did, not only in Sunday school, but also in a home setting with the family and other children.

> God's love for us is constant and never-ending. "He Himself has said, 'I will never leave you or forsake you'" (Hebrews 13:5).

The Apostle Paul made it clear in Romans 8:38–39 that nothing in all the universe, created or uncreated, "shall be able to separate us from the love of God which is in Christ Jesus our Lord."

The psalmist expressed his love for God's Word thusly: "The love of Your mouth is better to me than thousands of shekels of gold and silver" (Psalm 119:72). Adrian Rogers went so far as to say, "If you were to ask me to choose between a huge stack of gold, silver, rubies, diamonds, stocks, and bonds on the one hand or the Word of God on the other, I would not hesitate to choose the Word of God."

The question for you and me is, how much do we love the Word of God?

The Key: Meditation on God's Word

We've been emphasizing the timeless value and

treasured virtues of the Bible as being God's Amazing Love Letter of Forgiveness to all mankind. In it is God's will for our lives, and that's what we should be trying to understand as we read and meditate on the written Word of God.

I've heard more than one minister say that the number-one question they are asked—more than any other—is this: **What is God's will for my life?** And I find that to be true in my own life: "Lord, what do you want me to do? Please show me your will!" Dear reader, if you can relate to that desire in your own life—if you really want to know God's will for your life, I have some good news for you! You can find God's will by meditating on God's Word!

God created us to know Him and enjoy Him and center our lives on Him. He has a plan and a purpose for your life, and He wants to reveal it to you. As you diligently seek God's will by meditating on His Word, His answer comes through loud and clear: "Cease striving and *know that I am God*, I will be exalted among the nations, I will be exalted in the earth" (Psalm 46:10 NASB). Jesus Himself said, "*Ask*, and it will be given you, *seek* and you will find, *knock*, and it will be opened to you" (Luke 11:19). God reassured us when He spoke through the prophet, saying, "And you will seek Me and find Me when you search for Me with all your heart. I will be found by you, says the Lord" (Jeremiah 29:13–14a).

The Discipline of Meditation

To read God's Word effectively requires more than just casually reading it like a novel. I well remember the grind of studying in law school. Some of the smarter students were seemingly able to breeze through without apparently giving it much thought. But I was not that gifted. Not being one of the brighter students, I had to labor at it and spend much more time than most. It was not easy, but my extra time was worth the struggle. Maybe that's why I love meditating on the Word of God today. Evidently God had prepared me for my calling.

Here are five suggestions that I have found helpful in my own studying and meditating on the Bible. I hope they are of help to you:

1. **Make knowing God's Word your number-one priority**. If you really want to know what God is saying, He will help you. Why? Because to know Him and His Word is His highest priority for you as a believer. That's how He fulfills His number-one purpose of conforming you to the image and likeness of His Son. And that's why He tells you, "As newborn babies, desire the [pure] milk of the Word, that you may grow by it" (1 Peter 2:2). He also makes it clear that your responsibility is to "Draw near to God and He will draw near to you" (James 4:8). Meditation on God's Word is a cooperative effort: God will do His part by helping us understand, if we do our part by desiring it.

2. **Find a quiet place and a set time to read the Word**. This can be difficult for many of you, depending on your circumstances and stage in life. Being eighty-eight years old as this book goes to print and in the latter stages of my earthly existence, with an empty nest and a supportive wife, I am indeed blessed. The Lord made sure I had a home study for spending quiet time with Him. He also led me to

heed Benjamin Franklin's advice of "early to bed and early to rise . . ." In my case, 9 p.m. to 5 a.m. God said, "In quietness and confidence shall be your strength" (Isaiah 30:15). No matter how busy you are, the Lord will provide, if you sincerely desire it. Suzanna Wesley had eighteen children, among whom were John and Charles Wesley of Methodist fame. Her quiet time was found only to be under her apron pulled over her head.

3. **Make meditating on God's Word a daily routine.** Here again this can be difficult for many, especially if you are young with a busy job and/or growing family. But it can be done! The good part about establishing a daily routine is that when you break it (which we all do from time to time), we have something to come back to. During the holiday seasons, we all tend to be on a different schedule. I enjoy the change of pace, but am blessed to look forward to getting back to my usual routine. I'm well aware that some may think, "Ol' Dan is obsessed with the idea of reading the Bible and studying God's Word." They say I've gone overboard and have

become a religious fanatic. No, it's not religion we need; it's a working relationship with our Creator God and His Son that reveals the direction of our lives. As the psalmist says, "Your Word is a lamp to my feet and a light to my path" (Psalm 119:105).

4. **Journal your thoughts and His Word.** Back in October 1998 Margaret and I heard David Jeremiah speak at a three-day seminar at the Cove in Asheville, North Carolina. In one of his talks he described how journaling had become one of the great blessings of his life. He said he looked forward to it each day—just jotting down his thoughts as he sought God's will for his life. But what do you write (or type in his case)? He said, you can't go wrong. Whatever comes to mind, just write it down as if in an intimate conversation with the Lord Himself. So I decided to take him up on it, beginning January 1, 1999—and I've been doing it ever since—over twenty years now—and it has really been a blessing! It can be in the form of a prayer or a psalm, or just random thoughts. Lately I've been journaling God's Word. Why copy the Bible? Because "The grass withers, the

flower fades, but the Word of God stands forever" (Isaiah 40:5). It's His Love Letter to all mankind, and I highly recommend journaling it as you meditate on God's Word.

5. **Use reliable commentaries and devotionals for better understanding.** I have a number of commentaries, but the ones I use most are *The Believer's Bible Commentary* by William MacDonald, *The Moody Bible Commentary*, and Warren Wiersbe's two-volume *Expository Outlines on the Old and New Testament*. I found it also most helpful to journal MacDonald's commentary on Romans and other books of the Bible. I feel I can trust their considered thoughts, for each one is a seasoned and true man of God. Of course, there's nothing like letting God speak to you through your own reading and meditating on His Word. The three devotionals Margaret and I use together each morning are Sarah Young's *Jesus Calling* and *Dear Jesus*, as well as *My Utmost for His Highest* by Oswald Chambers. We get great joy and benefit from discussing these during our prayer time together each morning. We also use *Our Daily*

Bread as well as, from time to time, devotionals by Charles Stanley, David Jeremiah, Jack Graham, Adrian Rogers, and Michael Youssef.

These are just tools that I use, as well as some suggestions that may prove helpful to you. The Lord may lead you in an entirely different direction.

God wants all of His children to meditate on His Word. He told Joshua to "meditate in it day and night" (Joshua 1:8). It was a source of great joy for the psalmist: "Oh, how I love Your law! It is my meditation all the day" (Psalm 119:97).

Do you really want to know God's will for your life? I can't imagine anyone who doesn't! Then as Jesus said, "Ask and it will be given to you" (Luke 11:9). God promises, "If you ask anything in My name I will do it" (John 14:14). "You do not have because you do not ask" (James 4:2). Seeking and finding God's will for your life is a blessing beyond description. Jesus encourages you to "seek and you will find" (Luke 11:9).

"Is not My Word like a fire," says the
Lord, "And like a hammer that breaks
the rock in pieces?" (Jeremiah 23:29)

(The Word is like a hammer because of its
ability to tear down and build up.)

That He might sanctify and cleanse it
[the church] with the washing of water
by the Word. (Ephesians 5:26)

(The Word is called water because of its
cleansing, quenching, and refreshing quali-
ties.)

Here's a brief chapter-by-chapter review and synopsis of what this book is all about, and what I've tried to make known:

Chapter I: God wants all mankind to know who He is and who we are in relation to Him. He is the Creator and Sustainer of all life, including your life and mine. The Bible says He's the Creator of "the heavens and the earth," and He's in control. He rules over all. He's in charge of history. He wants us to know and accept how He has chosen to deal with man's sin of disobedience.

Chapter II: The Bible is the God-inspired Word of God, written in the words of men. It is infallible and inerrant. It is reliable, and it can be trusted in its entirety. Its overall theme is the redemption of sinful man through the blood sacrifice of God's only begotten Son, Jesus the Christ. It is one book containing sixty-six separate books, written by forty authors over a period of fifteen hundred years.

Chapter III: God wants us "to correctly handle" His Word of Truth by interpreting it from His perspective and in the context of His sovereign will and wisdom. He wants us to use Godly wisdom to interpret it literally in some parts and figuratively in other parts, depending on the circumstances and context in which it was originally written.

Chapter IV: God's Word has many aspects, but its overall theme is composed of Biblical Truths or Doctrines that teach us about sin and salvation, how to become a Christian, and how to live the Christian life. Three basic Doctrines emerge, the first of which is **Justification** (of the Spirit): how to have right standing with God. We are *justified by being born again*. We are saved, by God's grace through faith, for good works.

Chapter V: The second major Doctrine is **Sanctification**, which can be described as becoming in practice what we already are in position. When we are *Justified through faith*, we are saved from the death penalty of sin. That's our position in Christ. We then begin growing in Christ, our purpose being to become more like Christ. It's a life of ups and downs, of victories and defeats, all of which work together for God's glory!

Chapter VI: The third major Doctrine is **Glorification**, which is finally realized when our earthly existence is over and our bodies are resurrected. That's when we're in the very presence of our Lord and Savior. That's what all Christians can look forward to, and that's why there should be no fear of death, for we will be more alive then than we've ever been. That's the Truth and reality of eternal life!

Chapter VII: Our objective in reading God's Word should be to meditate on it on a consistent daily basis. God wants us to know the Truth of what He's trying to tell us. To appropriate His message of love and forgiveness requires developing the Godly habit of *prayer* and *thanksgiving* for God's goodness, and an increased *dependence on the work of the Holy Spirit*, and *greater faith in God.*

Chapter VIII: To benefit from meditating on

God's Word we must develop a life of obedience to His will. We need to know that we live in two different worlds: the physical world and the spiritual world. When you accept Jesus as your Lord and Savior, Christ comes into your life in the Person of the Holy Spirit. You belong to Him, and He has a Divine Purpose and Plan for your life.

Chapter IX: God's Word is "*living and powerful* and sharper than any two-edged sword." It's a living book, and you can make it come alive in your heart not just by reading it, but by meditating on it. In it is God's will for your life. The most important question you can ask God is, "Lord, what's your will for my life? What do you want me to do?" Then seek His leading to do His will.

What Did Jesus Believe about the Bible?

It's obvious that the only Scriptures Jesus could have known about were those of the Old Testament Law and the prophets. The New Testament had not been written during His lifetime.

The evidence is clear that Jesus upheld the law and lived by the law throughout His earthly existence. He did not come to destroy the law but to "fulfill it" (Matthew 5:17).

Jesus frequently referred to the historical accounts as recorded in the Old Testament. He obviously believed in Noah and the flood (Matthew 24:38) and in Jonah being "three days and three nights in the belly of the great fish" (Matthew 12:40). He made reference to the "wisdom of Solomon" (Matthew 12:42) and the "abomination of desolation" spoken of by the prophet Daniel (Matthew 24:15).

While walking on the road to Emmaus, Jesus joined two of His followers who were saddened and confused and not able to process what had really happened at the cross and the subsequent resurrection. Although they did not recognize Him, it was then that Jesus taught them a so-called master's-level course in Christian hermeneutics. Luke records,

"Then Jesus took them through the writings of Moses and all the prophets, explaining from all the Scripture the things concerning Himself" (Luke 24:2 NLT). The NLT footnote suggests that He in all likelihood took them through the suffering servant in Isaiah 53, the pierced one in Zechariah 12:10, and the message of the covenant in Malachi 3:1 (John the Baptist was the messenger who prepared the way for Jesus).

Jesus believed in the Old Testament Scriptures!

Jesus Taught That the Old Testament Scriptures Prophesied His Coming

In Luke 4:14–30 we learn that when Jesus returned in the power of the Holy Spirit to Galilee to begin the second year of His public ministry, His fame spread through all the surrounding region. As He taught in the Jewish synagogues, He was widely acclaimed. In Nazareth, His boyhood town, Jesus regularly went to the synagogue on the Sabbath day, Saturday. On one visit to the synagogue, He rose *to read* from the Old Testament Scriptures. The attendant handed Him the scroll on which Isaiah's prophecy was written. The Lord unrolled the scroll to what we now know as Chapter 61 of the book of Isaiah. He read verse 1 and the first half of verse 2. McDonald points out that this passage has always been acknowledged as a description of the ministry of the Messiah.

When Jesus said, "Today this Scripture is fulfilled in your hearing," He was saying in the clearest possible manner that He was the Messiah of Israel.

The Scripture Jesus read pointed to the Messiah's mission. He came to deal with the enormous problems that have affected mankind throughout history:

Poverty: "To preach the gospel to the poor."

Sorrow: "To heal the brokenhearted."

Bondage: "To proclaim liberty to the captives."

Suffering: "And recovery of sight to the blind."

Oppression: "To set at liberty those who are oppressed."

In short, "He came **to proclaim the acceptable year of the Lord.**"

Thus we see that Jesus not only knew and believed in the Old Testament writings of the law and prophets, but He preached them on a regular basis. Some were impressed by His gracious words, for it was a mystery to them how the son of Joseph the carpenter had developed so well.

But we learn from Luke 4:24–30 that others sought to "thrust Him out of the city, and they led Him to the brow of the hill … that they might throw Him down over the cliff." No doubt their thinking was instigated by Satan as another attempt to destroy God's Son. But Scripture says that Jesus miraculously walked through the crowd and left the city. His foes were powerless to stop Him, for His time had not yet come. All these events were orchestrated by the sovereign will of the God of the universe.

God Will Open Your Eyes of Understanding

If you are a child of God, it is His intended will that you come to understand His Written Word. Jesus opened the minds of His Emmaus Road disciples so that they could understand how the Old Testament Scriptures were all centered on Him as the long-awaited Messiah. Read what the Word says in Luke 24:45–47 (NLT):

> Then He *opened their minds to understand the Scriptures*. And He said, "Yes it is written long ago that the Messiah would suffer and die and rise from the dead on the third day. It was also written that this message would be proclaimed in the authority of His name to all nations, beginning in Jerusalem. There is forgiveness of sins for all who repent.

The Holy Spirit opens the minds of Christians today to understand the Scriptures. He will open your mind, if you *ask, seek, and knock* by studying and meditating on His Word. But be aware that "People who aren't spiritual [who aren't born again of the Spirit] can't receive these truths from God's Spirit. It all sounds foolish to them and they can't understand it, for only those who are spiritual can understand what the Spirit means" (1 Corinthians 2:14–15).

Are you born of the Spirit? Are you seeking to understand the Truth of God's will for your life? Are you meditating on His Word?

Gideons International and Its Statement about the Bible

The organization that has most promoted Bible reading throughout our society is Gideons International. In 1985 Gideons produced this statement concerning the Word of God:

> The Bible—it contains the mind of God, the state of man, the way of salvation, the doom of sinners, and the happiness of believers. Its doctrines are holy, its precepts are binding, its histories are true, and its decisions are immutable. Read it to be wise, believe it to be safe, practice it to be holy. It contains light to direct you, food to support you, and comfort to cheer you. It is the traveler's map, the pilgrim's staff, the pilot's compass, the soldier's sword, and the Christian's charter. Here paradise is restored, heaven opened, and the gates of hell disclosed. Christ is its grand subject, our good the design, and the glory of God its end. It should fill the memory, rule the heart, and guide the feet.

Read it slowly, frequently, and prayerfully. It is a mine of wealth, a paradise of glory, and a river of pleasure. It is given you in life, will be opened at the judgment, and be remembered forever. It involves the highest responsibility, will reward the greatest labor, and will condemn all who trifle with its sacred contents.

According to David Jeremiah's Study Bible:

The most beautiful statement of the trustworthiness of the Word of God is found in Psalm 19:7–11:

> The law of the Lord is perfect, converting the soul;
>
> The testimony of the Lord is sure, making wise the simple;
>
> The statutes of the Lord are right, rejoicing in the heart;
>
> The commandment of the Lord is pure, enlightening the eyes; …
>
> The judgments of the Lord are true and righteous altogether.…
>
> More to be desired are they than gold.…
>
> In keeping them there is great reward.

Perhaps the greatest testimony to the truthfulness of God's Word is its power to change the human heart (Hebrews 4:16). In a prayer to His Father, Jesus acknowledged that only Truth can sanctify (make holy), and that God's Word is the source of that Truth: "Sanctify them by Your Truth. Your Word is Truth" (John 17:17).

God's Word is true because God Himself is True and Truth!